Produced in partnership with

FIVE ESSENTIALS TO ENGAGE TODAY'S MEN

Conversations every church should have about how men connect with their purpose, with others & with their faith

Copyright © 2020 by Barna Group. All rights reserved.

ISBN: 978-1-945269-77-6

All information contained in this document is copyrighted by Barna Group and shall remain the property of Barna Group. U.S. and international copyright laws protect the contents of this document in their entirety. Any reproduction, modification, distribution, transmission, publication, translation, display, hosting or sale of all or any portion of the contents of this document is strictly prohibited without written permission of an authorized representative of Barna Group.

The information contained in this report is true and accurate to the best knowledge of the copyright holder. It is provided without warranty of any kind: express, implied or otherwise. In no event shall Barna Group or its respective officers or employees be liable for any special, incidental, indirect or consequential damages of any kind, or any damages whatsoever resulting from the use of this information, whether or not users have been advised of the possibility of damage, or on any theory of liability, arising out of or in connection with the use of this information.

Funding for this research was made possible by the generous support of BetterMan. Barna Group was solely responsible for data collection, analysis and writing of the report.

Contents

A Word from BetterMan   4

Introduction   5

1. Let's Talk About . . . Identity   7

2. Let's Talk About . . . Vocation   11

3. Let's Talk About . . . Well-Being   15

4. Let's Talk About . . . Relationships   19

5. Let's Talk About . . . Church   23

A Field Guide for Modern Men's Ministry   27

Methodology   30
Acknowledgments   31
About the Project Partners   32

A WORD FROM BETTERMAN

Ministry to men surged in the 1990s. Traditional roles for men seemed increasingly out of place and at odds with a rapidly changing modern world. In stadiums, churches and small group gatherings, men eagerly sought encouragement, affirmation and fresh spiritual direction. They were hungry for help. And many found it.

Unfortunately, much of this positive momentum and energy has now waned. A new generation of young men have now come into adulthood, and they are facing their own set of cultural challenges: significant changes in the workplace, the economy, family life and politics, alongside dramatic revisions in gender roles and expectations. This has led to terms like "toxic masculinity" and questions about the "feminization" of the Church.

Times have changed—and so has the cultural reframing of masculinity. Many men are enveloped by a masculine "fog." They need help—but what kind? Do we even know what's going on with men today?

To find out, we at BetterMan enlisted Barna to help us understand how we might build a 21st-century men's ministry capable of reaching churched, unchurched and de-churched men—particularly young men—with the transforming understanding of masculinity based on the person of Jesus and the teaching of the Bible.

What they found has informed, strengthened and confirmed our ministry at BetterMan. But even more, we believe these insights can help your church or the men's ministry you lead have a greater impact on men. That's our sincere desire in offering you these *Five Essentials to Engage Today's Men*.

BetterMan seeks to strengthen marriages, families and the community by helping men understand and live into the timeless and life-giving manhood of Jesus. Having conversations around these five critical areas of manhood will hopefully inspire us all.

TOM WILSON, BetterMan CEO
ROBERT LEWIS, BetterMan Founder

Introduction

What would it look like to bring men's ministry into the 21st-century? How would highly effective ministry to and among men be different today from 20 or 30 years ago? How would it account for the changing relationships between men and women in the workplace, the family and the Church?

Good answers to important questions about better ministry start with a hard look at the present. BetterMan, a resource for men's ministries, commissioned Barna to find out how both churchgoing Christians and men overall are navigating 21st-century waters. What researchers found are some undeniable shifts, generationally and otherwise, in how men are charting a way forward. Whether it's in their family, career, friendships or mental and spiritual health, men need each other—and the Church—to help them journey well.

This resource, *Five Essentials to Engage Today's Men*, is Barna's data-driven guidebook for men's ministries that are mapping their expedition into the future of manhood. Each brief chapter unpacks data on one essential aspect of men's lives—**identity, vocation, well-being, relationships** and **church engagement**—along with data visualizations that give contour to men's perspectives and experiences. Those five chapters are followed by a "field guide" to help you put the data into action in your own ministry.

The cultural ground is shifting beneath men's feet, but the scriptures offer solid ground on which to build a manhood for the 21st-century and beyond. We pray this resource will help as you guide men into the future God is preparing for them.

Definitions

All U.S. men is a nationally representative sample of male U.S. residents ages 18 and older. The group includes self-identified Christians, non-Christians and everyone in between.

Practicing Christians are self-identified Christians who have attended a worship service within the past month and agree strongly that their faith is very important in their life.

Non-Christians identify themselves as something other than Christian, including other religious faiths and "none of the above."

1

Let's Talk About . . . Identity

What makes Christian men who they are?

When asked to determine what aspects of their lives are core to their identity, four out of five practicing Christian men (80%) say their faith is central to how they see themselves. Unsurprisingly, this response is much higher among practicing Christians than among U.S. men overall (34%).

There are, in fact, several areas where practicing Christian men differ significantly from men overall and from non-Christian men in particular (see the chart on the following page). For example, practicing Christian men are considerably more likely to place their family at the core of their identity. Two of every five practicing Christian men (43%) say being a husband is central to their identity. The same proportion says being a father is at their core. (Check out chapter 4 for a breakdown of the important relationships in men's lives.) By comparison, only one-third of men in general considers being a husband (34%) or a father (35%) central to their identity. On the flip side, non-Christian men are more apt to place hobbies (26% vs. 13% practicing Christian men), career (25% vs. 13%) and financial status (23% vs. 13%) at the core of who they are. Practicing Christians are also more likely than non-Christians to say family traditions are central to who they are (34% vs. 29%).

Considering the emphasis churches often put on the family, it's not surprising that practicing Christians are more likely to elevate family alongside faith when it comes to their identity. What's more revealing is the path that leads many men to discover family's significance for them. While Christian men of all ages and stages place importance on family traditions, the significance of fatherhood only emerges once practicing Christian men have become one. Among Christian men who have never had children, fewer than one in six (15%) says becoming a father is central to their identity—but nearly six in 10 (57%) of those who have a child say being a father is core to who they are. This suggests that a desire to be a father

AT THE CORE OF WHO I AM

Where Men Plot Elements of Identity on a Target

◆ Practicing Christian men ◆ Non-Christian men

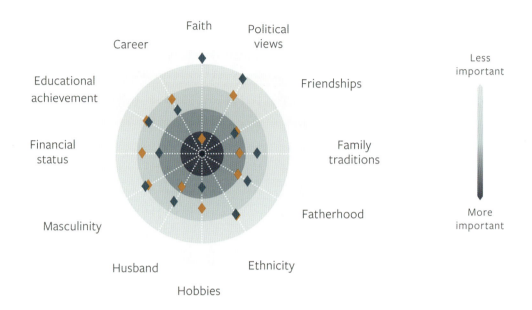

n=593 U.S. men 18 and older, 1,000 practicing Christian men 18 and older, October 8–21, 2019.
Respondents were invited to plot each value on a target like the one above. The values represented here are the mean for practicing Christians and non-Christians.

is not intrinsic to a majority of men early on, but becomes essential once they take on the role.

Beyond what practicing Christians believe about their individual identity, a large majority (67%) believes that masculinity as a whole is changing, far more than U.S. men overall (55%—note this is still a majority, albeit a slight one). Practicing Christians are likely dubious of the changes they believe are underway. Given a choice between two words that describe the state of masculinity today, Christian men are far more likely to choose the negative option. They're more likely to say masculinity is threatened rather than hopeful (44% vs. 31%), endangered rather than thriving (39% vs. 28%), confused rather than vibrant (47% vs. 26%), in crisis over stable (40% vs. 30%) and regressing over progressing (41% vs. 32%).

By contrast, U.S. men overall are less likely to say that masculinity today is confused (33%), threatened (29%), in crisis (29%), endangered (28%) or regressing (26%).

If practicing Christian men believe masculinity is changing, and largely believe those changes to be negative, the next question to consider is what factors they believe are responsible. When asked what factors, if any, oppose healthy masculinity, more than half of Christian men (54%) say the LGBTQ community

Let's Talk About...Identity

WORDS THAT DESCRIBE THE STATE OF MASCULINITY TODAY

◆ All U.S. men ◆ Practicing Christian men

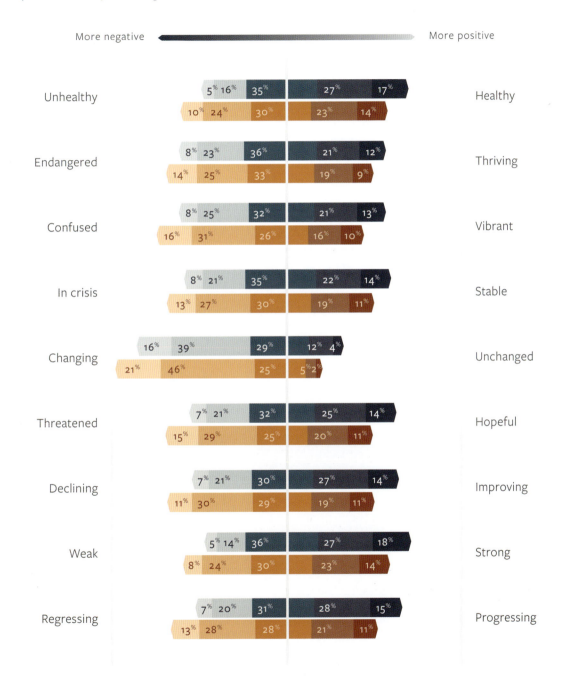

n=593 U.S. men 18 and older, 1,000 practicing Christian men 18 and older, October 8–21, 2019.

> A large majority of practicing Christian men believes that masculinity as a whole is changing

is a source of opposition. A similar percentage (53%) says healthy masculinity is under threat from unrealistic portrayals of men in media. Just under half credit liberalism (46%) and feminism (45%) as in opposition to masculinity.

Young Christian men differ considerably from their older brothers in faith. Christian men under 35 are significantly less likely (38%) to think the LGBTQ community opposes healthy masculinity than Christian men 35 to 54 (55%) and 55 and older (61%), and more prone to cite toxic masculinity as a source of opposition (48% vs. 38% and 39%, respectively). There is also a sharp difference between age groups when it comes to views about the future of masculinity. Young men under 35 are significantly more likely to be hopeful about masculinity's future (69%) compared to men 35 to 54 (55%) and 55 and older (46%).

This is important because practicing Christian men who express hope about the future of masculinity are more likely to score highly on a measure of overall satisfaction (64%) compared to those who are either neutral on the subject (50%) or are not hopeful about the future of masculinity (43%). ♦

OUR CULTURAL MOMENT
GENERATIONAL DIFFERENCES ON MORAL QUESTIONS

Older and younger generations not only disagree about the state of masculinity today, they also disagree on a number of moral issues, such as those related to personal sexual behavior. Just over one-third of practicing Christian men under 35 (37%) says they believe sex before marriage is always morally wrong. By comparison, half of Christian men between 35 and 54 (50%) believe this is true. Not unrelated is the fact that, among Christian men who are in a serious relationship or casually dating, one-third (33%) is living with his significant other. This is equal to the percentage of U.S. men overall (32%). Looking at other social and sexual issues, Christian men under 35 are nearly twice as likely to say that viewing pornography is rarely or never wrong (32% vs. 17% all 35 and older). Younger Christians are also less likely to say that homosexuality is always wrong compared to older generations (42% vs. 60% 35 to 54, 54% 55 and older) and twice as likely to say abortion is rarely or never wrong (21% vs. 10% all 35+).

2

Let's Talk About . . . Vocation

In almost every conversation between strangers, there are two questions that get things going: *What's your name?* and *What do you do?* In our cultural imagination, our job is nearly on the same level as our name when it comes to identity. Barna wanted to know whether this perception of vocational identity carries over to the lived experience of practicing Christian men. As we saw in the previous chapter, career *is* important, but for most Christians it is not *central* to their identity.

Let's start with the basics. Half of practicing Christian men (50%) are employed full-time while approximately one-third (31%) is retired. The remainder are split between part-time employment (10%) and unemployment (10%). Men under 35 are significantly more likely to say they are employed part-time (21%) or that they are unemployed and looking for work (16%).

When asked about their career goals, nearly two-thirds of practicing Christian men (62%) say their goal is to do something they love, in line with U.S. men overall (63%). However, beyond doing something they love, practicing Christians differ sharply from men in general. Christians are significantly more likely to say they are seeking a healthy work-personal life balance (63% vs. 52% all men) and half cite "making a difference" as their career goal (50% vs. 37% all men). By contrast, two out of every five men

MEN'S CAREER GOALS

% among men who are working or looking for work; respondents could select up to three.

◆ All U.S. men ◆ Practicing Christian men

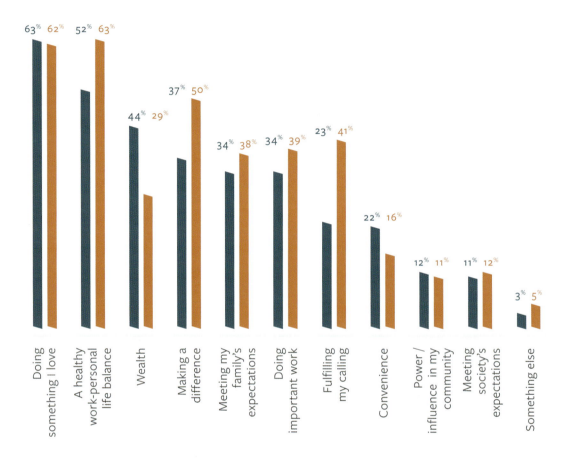

n=420 U.S. men 18 and older, 689 practicing Christian men 18 and older, October 8–21, 2019.

overall (42%) identify wealth as their career goal, compared to 30 percent of Christian men.

Career hyperfocus is a problem for some men. Among U.S. men who report feeling overwhelmed at some point in the past month, one-third says their career is central to their identity (34%), compared to one in five of those who rarely or never feel overwhelmed (19%). There is an opportunity here for men's ministries to provide coaching and guidance about where career fits into a godly, healthy life.

Practicing Christian men who report feeling overwhelmed frequently or sometimes in the last month are more likely than other Christian men to say their career goals include either wealth (35% vs. 23% who rarely or never feel overwhelmed) or to fulfill their calling (45% vs. 37%). Those who rarely or never feel

> Christian men are seeking a healthy work-personal life balance

overwhelmed are more likely to say that having a healthy work-personal life balance is a goal for their work (67% vs. 58% who frequently or sometimes feel overwhelmed).

Half of practicing Christian men who are currently employed report feeling satisfied with their career (23% very + 31% mostly). This is considerably higher than among men overall, where about two in five say they are satisfied (24% very + 24% mostly).

One in four Christian men (26%) says they are very satisfied with the balance between their work and life, and an additional one-third (31%) says they are mostly satisfied. Considering the added stressors that can come from family life, it's interesting that practicing Christians who are married are considerably more likely to report satisfaction with their work-life balance compared to those who are unmarried. Nearly two-thirds of husbands report being either very

OUR CULTURAL MOMENT
GENDER ROLES, STAY-AT-HOME PARENTING & GENDER EQUALITY

Practicing Christian men are more likely than non-Christians to say they are comfortable with women adhering to traditional gender roles like caring for children and family (49% agree strongly or somewhat vs. 37% among non-Christians). Similarly, non-Christian men are more likely to say they disagree with these roles (29% vs. 19%).

However, two-thirds of practicing Christian men (65% agree strongly or somewhat) say it is important to encourage gender equality. Unsurprisingly, young men are more likely (76%) to say so compared to older Christians (63% 35 to 54, 61% 55 and older). Similarly, three-quarters of all practicing Christian men (78%) believe it is okay for a man to be a stay-at-home parent. This time, however, young Christian men are *less* likely to agree (68%) than Christian men 35 to 54 (82%) or 55 and older (79%).

In many workplaces, men have an opportunity to interact with women outside of their family. Three-quarters of practicing Christian men have had a woman coworker (78%) and six in 10 have worked under a female boss (62%). Those who agree they are more comfortable with women in traditional gender roles are less likely to have had a female boss (53%) than Christians who disagree (73%). Pessimism about masculinity is correlated with having had a female boss or coworker, indicating that some Christian men need healthy tools to navigate these professional relationships.

or mostly satisfied with work-life balance (29% very + 34% mostly) compared to fewer than half of single Christians (20% very + 27% mostly). Having a family appears to provide married men with a reason to disconnect from work (or at least something else to connect to) that single men don't have, especially as the latter are typically younger, delaying marriage and in a season centered around career-building.

3

Let's Talk About . . . Well-Being

When practicing Christian men are asked about their level of satisfaction in 13 different areas of life—from their marriage and friendships to their feelings about the future—more than half (56%) are very or mostly satisfied overall. Another three in 10 (29%) are somewhat satisfied.

While overall satisfaction is, of course, ideal, data reveal some notable trends when it comes to specific areas of life. Asked about satisfaction with their mental health, three-quarters of Christian men say they are very (45%) or mostly (28%) satisfied. Men 55 and older, however, are significantly more likely (82%) to report satisfaction with mental health than those 35 to 54 (69%) or under 35 (62%)—and since older men compose about half (47%) of all practicing Christian men, this divergence suggests some significant issues among younger generations.

A similar trend can be found in the realm of spiritual health. Three-quarters of Christian men report being very (42%) or mostly (35%) satisfied with their spiritual health, but again those 55 and older are significantly more likely to express satisfaction (87% very + mostly) than the younger age cohorts (72% 35 to 54; 63% under 35). It's possible this uptick in mental and spiritual health among older men is related to a corresponding uptick in satisfaction with the lighter schedule that may come in later years. Seven out of 10 Christian men 55 and older (31% very + 39% mostly) report being satisfied with the leisure and rest they are getting, while only around half of those 35 to 54 (53%) and men under 35 (46%) report satisfaction in this area.

With these responses in mind, it's notable that young Christian men (55%) are significantly more likely to say they have frequently or occasionally felt lonely within the last month,

PRACTICING CHRISTIANS REPORT GREATER SATISFACTION IN VARIOUS AREAS OF LIFE

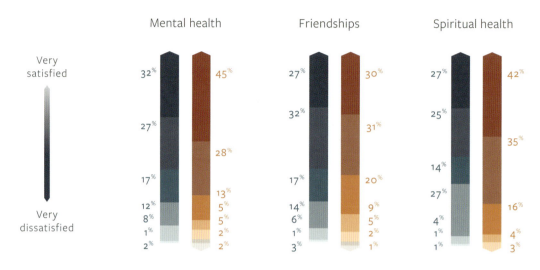

n=593 U.S. men 18 and older, 1,000 practicing Christian men 18 and older, October 8–21, 2019.

compared to older men (28% 55 and older; 43% 35 to 54). (Remember that Christian men over 35 are more likely to be married, and married men are significantly less likely to experience loneliness than those who are single, 29% vs. 57%—so marital status almost certainly plays a part here.)

OUR CULTURAL MOMENT
A PROFILE OF THE LONELY

More than one-third of practicing Christian men (38%) reports feeling lonely at least occasionally within the past month. Those who say so are more likely than average to be under 35, among whom more than half (55%) have struggled with loneliness, and never to have been married (59%).

Those who belong to ethnic minorities are more likely to struggle with loneliness (48%). In particular, more than half of black Christian men (54%) report recent struggles with loneliness, compared to one-third of white men (34%).

Those who consider themselves to be politically liberal are more likely than conservatives to say they struggle with loneliness (49% vs. 35%).

Those who lack a confidant (57%) and those who say technology is a source of social isolation (45%) are also more likely to report having felt lonely in the past month.

PRACTICING CHRISTIANS REPORT GREATER SATISFACTION IN VARIOUS AREAS OF LIFE, CONT'D

◆ All U.S. men ◆ Practicing Christian men

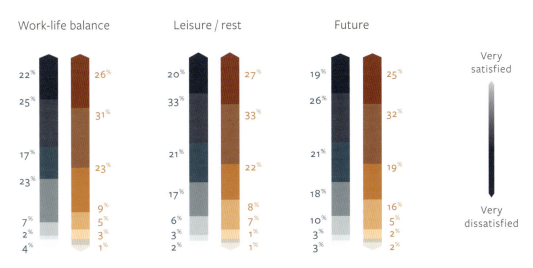

n=593 U.S. men 18 and older, 1,000 practicing Christian men 18 and older, October 8–21, 2019.

Similarly, just one-quarter of Christian men 55 and older (23%) reports frequent or occasional issues with being overwhelmed while half of those 35 to 54 (50%) and two-thirds of those under 35 say so (69%).

Struggles with loneliness and feeling overwhelmed have a marked impact on overall satisfaction. Just one-third of Christian men who struggle with loneliness (33%) or being overwhelmed (37%) is very or mostly satisfied with their life overall, compared to seven in 10 who do *not* struggle with these issues.

Perhaps relatedly, satisfaction scores are dramatically higher among practicing Christian men who say they have a confidant other than their partner or spouse (62% vs. 34% among those who do not have a confidant). Likewise, those who report rarely or never feeling lonely are significantly more likely to say they have a confidant (84% vs. 65% among those who frequently or occasionally feel lonely). The same dynamic holds between those who rarely or never feel

> Young Christian men are significantly more likely than older Christians to have felt lonely within the last month

overwhelmed (84% have a confidant) compared to those who frequently or occasionally feel lonely (66%).

While practicing Christian men appear to be doing well overall, it is clear there are opportunities to improve their mental, spiritual and emotional well-being—and the presence of strong communal ties is directly connected to satisfaction in these areas. ◆

4

Let's Talk About . . . Relationships

From marriage to parenthood to friendship, relationships shape the way everyone, including men, experiences life. However, the particular shape of those relationships differs for practicing Christian men compared to men overall. First and foremost, practicing Christian men are far more likely to be married. Two-thirds (67%) report they are married, compared to four in 10 U.S. men (41%); they are more than twice as likely to be married than non-Christian men (31%). Practicing Christians are likewise more likely to marry early, with roughly two in five (43%) marrying under the age of 25, compared to just one-third of non-Christian men overall (34%).

When it comes to divorce and cohabitation, however, there are few differences between practicing Christians and the U.S. average. More than one-quarter of Christian men (28%) who have been married has also experienced a divorce, which is on par with U.S. men in general. Moreover, practicing Christian men (33%) who are not married are just as likely as men overall to be living with their significant other (32%).

THE CONNECTION BETWEEN HAVING A CONFIDANT & MEN'S WELL-BEING

% very satisfied among practicing Christian men

♦ Has confidant   ♦ Does not have confidant

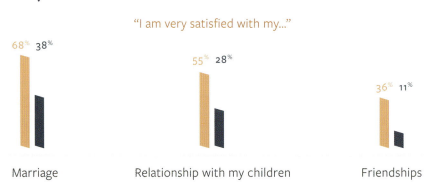

"I am very satisfied with my…"

Marriage	Relationship with my children	Friendships
68% / 38%	55% / 28%	36% / 11%

THE CONNECTION BETWEEN INTERGENERATIONAL FRIENDSHIPS & MEN'S WELL-BEING

% very satisfied among practicing Christian men

♦ Has friends of a different age group   ♦ No intergenerational relationships

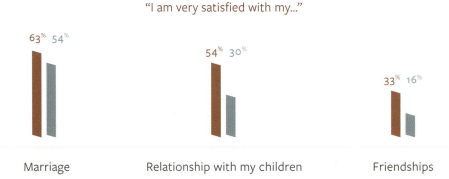

"I am very satisfied with my…"

Marriage	Relationship with my children	Friendships
63% / 54%	54% / 30%	33% / 16%

n=1,000 practicing Christian men 18 and older, October 8–21, 2019.

Among practicing Christians who are married, men between 35 to 54 years old are less likely than those in other age cohorts (49% vs. 70% under 35; 67% 55 and older) to say they are very satisfied in their marriage. At the same time, they are also more likely to have children under 18 living in their homes and to be employed full-time—both of which may put pressure on a marriage. Nearly half of practicing Christian men between 35 and 54 (47%) have children in their household, compared to just one-third of Christian men under 35 (37%) and few who are 55 and older (5%). Three-quarters of middle-age Christians work full-time (73%), more than both younger (59%) and older (29%) Christian men.

Christian fathers largely report satisfaction with their relationship with their children. Half (49%) say

> Intergenerational friendships tend to correlate with greater overall relationship satisfaction

they are very satisfied while another three in 10 (30%) say they're mostly satisfied. Not surprisingly, Christian men who report a positive relationship with their father growing up are considerably more likely to say they are very satisfied in their relationship to their own child (53%) compared to those whose relationship with their father was not positive (42%). Christian men who report having a confidant other than their partner or spouse are twice as likely to report being very satisfied in the area of fatherhood (55%) compared to those who have no such confidant (28%). This is a huge opportunity for men's ministries that can connect dads with mentors and friends.

Friendship plays an important role in the lives of all practicing Christian men, but it's a much larger role among those under 35 and 55 and older than those in middle age. Young men (34%) and older men (32%) are more likely than those between 35 and 54 (25%) to say they are very satisfied with their friendships. On the flip side, younger men are also three times more likely than those who are older to express dissatisfaction with their friendships (16% vs. 5%), hinting

OUR CULTURAL MOMENT
#METOO AND PAST TREATMENT OF WOMEN

Over the past few years, the #MeToo movement has become a cultural force. When asked about it, more than one in five practicing Christian men (22%) says they believe it is necessary in order to address mistreatment of women. Slightly more (29%) say the movement is an overcorrection and poses harm to men. A bit more than one in three (38%) goes so far as to say #MeToo opposes healthy masculinity, but there is strong disagreement among age groups here: Younger men (26%) are considerably less likely than older men (44%) to agree that #MeToo and healthy masculinity are in opposition.

Nearly half of practicing Christian men (44%) say they have treated a woman in a way that, looking back, they regret (though this survey did not allow them to specify the nature of that treatment). Those who say their views on masculinity have changed either a lot or somewhat over time are considerably more likely to say so (62%). Similarly, those who say the #MeToo movement is necessary are also more likely to regret the way they treated women (50%), compared to men who believe the movement is an overcorrection (41%).

at the problems, also uncovered elsewhere, of loneliness among young men.

Friendships, especially intergenerational friendships, tend to correlate with greater overall relationship satisfaction. Practicing Christian men who report having intergenerational friendships with both older and younger men are nearly twice as likely to be very satisfied in their relationship with their child (54% vs. 30%) and in their marriage (64% vs. 54%). ◆

5

Let's Talk About . . . Church

Most discussions about church engagement start with a simple question: *Who is in the pews?* Just under half of practicing Christian men (47%) are 55 and older, with an additional one-third (34%) between the ages of 35 and 54. The remainder are under the age of 35 (20%).

The age split among non-churchgoers is inverted, with nearly half of non-Christian men under the age of 35 (47%), one-third between 35 and 54 (32%) and just one in five over the age of 55 (20%).

There is a silver lining: Young church-going Christian men *mean it* when it comes to church. While those under 35 are less likely to be practicing Christians, the ones who *are* involved in church are more likely than older generations to engage in church-related activities. Nearly three-quarters (72%) have attended a small group or Bible study in the past month, compared to just over half of men 35 to 54 (54%) and two in five men 55 or older (40%). They are also more likely to be involved in community service projects (46% vs. 29% 35 and older), to attend Christian seminars and workshops (48% vs. 24%) and to participate in mentoring by either mentoring someone else (42% vs. 27%) or receiving mentoring themselves (41% vs. 13%). Young men who stay connected to the Church are among the most invested.

Why are practicing Christian men in church? Nearly nine out of 10 (88%) say it's in order to grow their faith. Two-thirds (68%) say they're in church to learn how the scriptures apply to their lives. About half indicate they attend because it is important to be involved with the community (54%).

There are some important generational differences when it comes to the *whys* of church. Younger men are less likely than average to attend for scriptural application (49%). On the other hand, they are *more* apt to say they're in church for mentoring (27% vs. 14% 35 and older), for leadership opportunities (28% vs. 21%) and for access to vocational training (15% vs. 4% 35 and older).

Among all practicing Christian men, one-third (32%) has participated in a men's ministry small group or program in the last year. Men under 55 (37%) are more likely to have participated in a men's ministry compared to those over 55 (27%). Among those who participated in some form of men's ministry, seven in 10 (71%) report a very positive experience.

More than half of those who did not participate in a men's ministry during the past year report at least some interest (15% definitely + 41% probably), while another three in 10 say they are not interested (24% probably not + 6% definitely not). Just six in 10 practicing Christian men (57%) report their church offers some type of men's small group or Bible study. A slightly smaller percentage (48%) says their church offers counseling for men and about one-third (35%) indicates that leadership training is available for men.

> Young men who stay connected to the Church are among the most invested in the Church

OUR CULTURAL MOMENT
PEACE, REST & HOPE: WHAT CHURCHES CAN OFFER NON-CHRISTIAN MEN

Non-Christian men have a range of needs that churches are well-positioned to meet. They are less likely than practicing Christians to be very satisfied with their mental health (28% vs. 45%) and spiritual health (25% vs. 42%), indicating a deep need for restoration and growth in these areas. They are significantly more likely to report frequently or sometimes feeling lonely (52% vs. 38%).

Given these struggles, it's unsurprising that non-Christian men are also less likely to be satisfied when it comes to leisure / rest (47% vs. 60%), work-life balance (45% vs. 58%) and their view of the future (39% vs. 56%). Churches can help bring peace to men battling overwork and anxiety—especially young non-Christian men, who are struggling most of all.

THE CONNECTION BETWEEN MEN'S MINISTRY & MEN'S WELL-BEING

% very satisfied among practicing Christian men

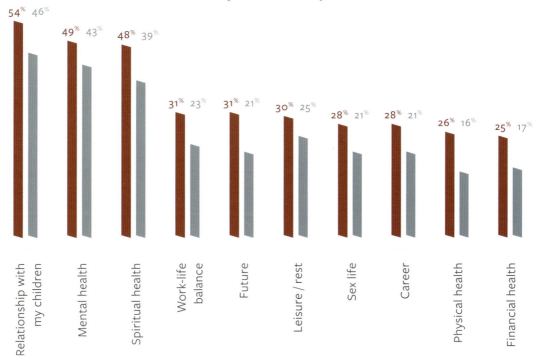

n=1,000 practicing Christian men 18 and older, October 8–21, 2019.

Younger men are more likely to report their church offers classes or seminars on the topic of masculinity (26% vs. 21% 35 to 54, 11% 55 and older), sports teams (28% vs. 20% 35 and older) arts or musical groups (25% vs. 18% 35 and older) and vocational or career assessment (19% vs. 10% 35 to 54, 5% 55 and older). This may indicate either that younger men are attracted to churches that offer such opportunities or that they are more aware than older men of such offerings.

Do men's ministries impact the people who participate in them? Two-thirds of men who participated in a men's ministry in the last year report they are very or mostly satisfied with their work-life balance (63% very + mostly), compared to only half who did not participate in a men's ministry (54%). Fathers who participated in men's ministries are more likely to be very satisfied with their relationship with their child (54%) compared to those who did not (46%). Even if men's ministries do not turn bad relationships good, they appear to have some effect at turning good ones into something even better.

A Field Guide for Modern Men's Ministry

Now that we've explored the findings, it's time to do something with them—to turn information into wisdom, data into action. Here are some questions to get you started. Think them through in prayer with your team.

Prioritize the five essentials according to the needs of your guys, rather than taking on everything at once. Effective ministry to, for and with men is a marathon, not a 100-yard dash—forming men in the image of Christ takes both time and prayerful intention.

Consider partnering with other churches or ministries in your area, especially if you're on the front end of launching or relaunching a men's ministry. It can be easier to create momentum and critical mass with pooled resources and collaboration.

Speaking of collaboration, team with women's ministry leaders. You'll get a fuller picture of what's happening across your community and better understand points of pain and disconnection. And together, you can align your efforts to grow disciples in the same direction.

Finally, lean hard into intergenerational ministry. In study after study, data show the power of these kinds of relationships to reduce loneliness and alienation and to create and sustain a sense of mutual, meaningful belonging. Both older and younger men may need help connecting—culturally, we're all out of the habit—so think about what you can do to help them forge these bonds.

May God bless you as you engage men in pursuit of Jesus.

IDENTITY

♦ Practicing Christian men are more likely than U.S. men overall to believe masculinity is under threat today and to be pessimistic about the future of masculinity. How can men's ministry leaders respond to the cultural changes men are experiencing? What can your church do to help and support those who are feeling unsettled or displaced? How can you guide men to a healthy understanding of masculinity?

♦ There is a clear divide between younger and older generations when it comes to almost all aspects of faith. Not only are young men less likely to go to church, but even those who do practice faith are apt to disagree with their elders when it comes to moral issues—especially those related to sex. Should churches adapt to these generational changes? If so, how? How can your ministry work to bridge these divides?

NOTES

VOCATION

◆ Men who pursue wealth or focus on career success are more likely to feel lonely and overwhelmed. How can your ministry help men slow down, find a balance between work and life and resist the desire to hustle and get ahead in their careers?

◆ On the other hand, men who are experiencing difficulties or disruptions in their careers, especially those who are unemployed or working part-time, are also more likely to feel overwhelmed and lonely, and less likely to say they are satisfied in their lives. How can you support men who are going through trying economic times? Could your ministry equip older men to help those in younger generations, who are more likely to report these struggles?

WELL-BEING

◆ Men are desperately in need of meaningful relationships. Those who lack in relational areas of life, whether family or close friends, are far more likely to be less satisfied in their lives and to feel lonely and overwhelmed. How can your ministry foster connections among these men who are disconnected from the rest of the community? How can your church be a source of support and encouragement for those who are struggling to find community? What tools can you offer them to build stronger relationships and overcome their social isolation?

◆ Non-Christian men, especially young men, are particularly likely to experience a lack of community and connection. How can you reach out to offer community and emotional support for this group? What are some ways your church can reach out to young men, especially single young men, who are struggling for connection in our society?

RELATIONSHIPS

◆ Churches in America have long placed a heavy emphasis on marriage and family, so it is not surprising that far more practicing Christian men than non-Christians are married. This raises two seemingly opposite questions for churches. First, how is your church encouraging healthy marriages and families now and how can you share these tools with more people?

NOTES

Second, what are you doing to welcome single men? What can you do to reach out to young single men and help them feel wanted and fulfilled, whether or not they ever get married?

◆ The relationship between a man and his dad when he was growing up appears to be a powerful predictor of his own mental health and overall satisfaction with life. With this in mind, how can your ministry support and strengthen the relationships between fathers today and their own children, who comprise the Church's next generation?

CHURCH

◆ There is a clear connection between men's participation in men's ministries and their overall satisfaction with life, from their marriage to their children to their work-life balance. However, the cause of this connection is not clear. Are men more likely to find satisfaction in the rest of their lives because of what they experience in men's ministries, or are the men who seek out these ministries already living satisfied lives, thus allowing them the freedom to participate? If men in *your* ministry are indeed more satisfied because of their participation, what specific tools are you giving them to improve their relationships? Can your church put these tools into the hands of even more men? How?

◆ Churches would also be wise to note how different generations get involved in the church. Middle-aged and older men make up a much larger percentage of men in the pews, but younger men are more likely to get involved in other ways. It's also clear that intergenerational friendships, mentors and confidants have a great impact on men's lives. How can churches create more opportunities for younger men and older men to form intergenerational friendships and thus support each other as part of the church?

Methodology

The research for this study consisted of two online surveys conducted October 8–21, 2019, with 1,593 U.S. men (1,000 practicing Christians and 593 from among the general U.S. population).

Practicing Christians self-identify as Christian, say their faith is very important in their life and have attended church within the past month (other than for a service or for a special event, such as a wedding or a funeral). The margin of error for this sample is plus or minus 2.9 percent at the 95-percent confidence level. The margin of error for the general population of men is plus or minus 3.9 percent at the 95-percent confidence level.

Researchers set quotas to obtain a minimum readable sample by a variety of demographic factors and weighted the two samples by region, ethnicity, education and age to reflect their natural presence in the population (using U.S. Census Bureau data for comparison). Partly by nature of using an online panel, these respondents are slightly more educated than the average American, but Barna researchers adjusted the representation of college-educated individuals in the weighting scheme accordingly.

Acknowledgments

BetterMan wants to acknowledge the contributions of several individuals responsible for making this project possible: Mark Matlock for initiating and managing the project; Barry Davis, Matt Levy, Austin Adams and Robert Lewis for supporting the project as BetterMan's board of directors. Thanks to Dave Travis, Russell Rainey and David Pinkerton for their contributions as advisors and contributors to the content and early analysis. Finally, thanks to BetterMan Summit attendees who provided initial feedback on the data: Authentic Manhood, National Coalition of Men's Ministry, The Core, Man in The Mirror, Iron Sharpens Iron and New Canaan Society, with special appreciation to Mike Young, James Anderson, Tim Phillips, Brian Doyle and Rick Caldwell.

The Barna team is deeply grateful to our partners at BetterMan. The researchers for *Five Essentials to Engage Today's Men* were David Kinnaman, Brooke Hempell, Traci Hochmuth, Aidan Dunn, Daniel Copeland and Pam Jacob. Under the editorial direction of Alyce Youngblood, Benjamin Howard and Aly Hawkins wrote the report. Doug Brown edited the manuscript. Annette Allen designed the cover and the report. Brenda Usery managed production with project management assistance from Elissa Clouse. The *Five Essentials* team thanks our Barna colleagues Amy Brands, Kristin Jackson, Joe Jensen, Savannah Kimberlin, Steve McBeth, Rhesa Storms, Verónica Thames, Jess Villa and Todd White.

About the Project Partners

Barna Group is a research firm dedicated to providing actionable insights on faith and culture, with a particular focus on the Christian church. In its 35-year history, Barna has conducted more than one million interviews in the course of hundreds of studies, and has become a go-to source for organizations that want to better understand a complex and changing world from a faith perspective.

Barna's clients and partners include a broad range of academic institutions, churches, nonprofits and businesses, such as Alpha, the Templeton Foundation, Fuller Seminary, the Bill and Melinda Gates Foundation, Maclellan Foundation, DreamWorks Animation, Focus Features, Habitat for Humanity, The Navigators, NBC-Universal, the ONE Campaign, Paramount Pictures, the Salvation Army, Walden Media, Sony and World Vision. The firm's studies are frequently quoted by major media outlets such as *The Economist*, BBC, CNN, *USA Today*, the *Wall Street Journal*, Fox News, Huffington Post, *The New York Times* and the *Los Angeles Times*.

www.Barna.com

BetterMan is a growing community of men who desire a better, more fulfilling life from our work, families, friends, marriages and from our relationships with God. The BetterMan framework actively seeks to counter today's dysfunctional masculinity by offering men the timeless, life-giving manhood found in the Bible. Our mission is to activate men's lives to a *better* masculinity; one that lifts up others, builds up others and gives life to others. This is the true masculinity God designed from the beginning.

At BetterMan, our passion is to help men discover and implement that design.

www.BetterMan.com